Plan in a Can!™
Fall and Winter Theme
4th-5th Grades

Full Day Emergency Sub Plans

by Eve Drueke

Find more ready-made lesson plans from Eve Drueke at Amazon.com

Check out even more original learning materials, games,
and printable books at www.myplaninacan.com.

How to Use Plan in a Can!

Use **Plan in a Can!** when you're...

sick and
need a sub

...out for workshops
or meetings

...or tired of the
same old materials!

All you have to do is...

1. Make copies
using the Copyroom
Quick Guide.

2. Take a moment to
indicate your preferences
for the substitute.

3. Relax!
You're done!

Enjoy the peace of mind of knowing your students are
engaged in high-interest, meaningful learning activities from
Plan in a Can!

Plan in a Can!: 4-5th Grades: Fall and Winter Theme
Table of Contents

A Note from Eve Drueke

Dear Educator,

Thank you so much for your purchase of **Plan in a Can! Fall and Winter Theme: 4th-5th Grades**.

If you're like I am, you've spent too many evenings preparing sub plans before a sick day or teachers' workshop, wishing you already had a set of ready-made plans to leave for a substitute. At last, I created plans that are clear, ready to use, and full of relevant content and learning activities. Everything is already done for you, including directions for substitute teachers, answer keys, and even helpful forms about vital classroom information for you to fill out, if you choose. If you're in a real pinch, there's even a **Copyroom Checklist** to indicate which printables you need to have copied.

Plan in a Can! includes many printables and activities that can be used again and again. Your purchase entitles you to unlimited use within your own classroom. Please, respect my work and follow copyright law by refraining from distributing these materials outside of your classroom.

I hope you find this ready-made kit useful, engaging, and time-saving! Extra time is a precious commodity in a teacher's life--enjoy getting a little back by opening a **Plan in a Can!**

Many more of my original lessons, mini-books, and learning activities from are available online at:

www,amazon.com
www.myplaninacan.com

Thank you again for your purchase.

Happy Teaching!
Eve Drueke

2

Important Classroom Information

Vital Information

Emergency procedures and information can be found:

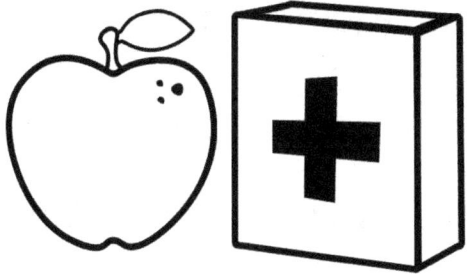

_____

Please note the following students with medical conditions:

Student	Condition	Notes

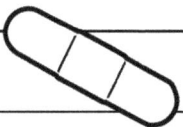

Important Phone Numbers:

Main Office	
Nurse	

Additional Notes

_____

_____

_____

3

Our Morning Routine:

☐ Students will come in on their own. ☐ Pick students up from _____ at: __:___

When students enter the classroom, they should:

_____

_____

_____

_____

Take attendance by:

_____

_____

Take lunch count by:

_____

_____

Classroom Management:

Our classroom discipline plan:

_____

_____

_____

_____

Extra-reliable students include:

_____

_____

Students who may need additional support following classroom expectations include:

_____

_____

4

Schedule Details

The following students will leave the classroom:

Student	Time	Destination	Notes

End of Day Procedures

☐ _____

☐ _____

☐ _____

☐ _____

☐ _____

☐ _____

Before you leave, please:

_____

_____

Additional Notes:

_____

_____

_____

_____

Today's Schedule: _____

Time	Activity	Notes

Lesson Plans: Plan in a Can!™ 4th and 5th Grades

A. Fall Festival Math Practice, Start Time_____, End Time_____

In this activity, students will solve word problems, using a variety of mathematical operations.

Distribute the copies of the **Fall Festival Math Practice** (3 pages). This packet is a mixture of word problems, fractions, division, and multiplication. Remind students to read the word problems very carefully and show their work on their own paper. Please circulate and help as needed.

Students who may require additional support: _____

Additional Notes: _____

_____

B. Secret Code Multiplication and Division, Start Time_____, End Time_____

In this activity, students will solve multiplication and division problems in order to complete the code and reveal the answer to winter riddles.

Distribute the **Secret Code Multiplication and Division** worksheet and briefly cover directions with the class. Stuents may not use calculators.

Students who may require additional support: _____

Additional Notes: _____

_____

C. Scrambled Sentences Paragraph Activity, Start Time_____, End Time_____

In this activity, students will "unscramble" a set of sentences that have been placed out of order. When the sentences are placed in the correct order, they will create a three-paragraph essay about hedgehogs.

1. Read the directions out loud with the students. Emphasize that the topic sentence of each paragraph often introduces the ideas in the rest of the paragraph, and the topic paragraph gives a "sneak peak" at what the rest of the essay will say.

2. The introductory paragraph may be the most difficult to assemble. Students can work in any order, but should be sure to read each sentence very carefully.

3. Have students carefully cut out each sentence strip, and be careful not to lose scraps or sentences on the floor.

4. Students should then begin to arrange the sentences into three paragraphs by grouping them in a logical order. A few sentences may make sense in more than one place. Students should use their best judgment about where sentences make the most sense.

Lesson Plans, continued

5. Students should glue the sentences to a sheet of paper once they are CERTAIN their paragraphs are in a logical order. They should not "glue as they go". Remind students to re-read their paragraphs as they work to ensure that the order of sentences make sense and similar ideas are grouped together.

6. Please remind students to put their names on the completed sheets and clean up all paper scraps from the floor.

Students who may require additional support:_____

Additional Notes:_____

D. "Sweet History: The Story of Hot Chocolate" Reading Activity, Start Time_____, End Time_____

In the following activity, students will read a passage on the history of hot chocolate and answer comprehension questions.

1. The "Sweet History" passage should be read (choose one):

☐ independently ☐ with assigned partners ☐ with student-chosen partners

☐ in small groups ☐ as a whole class

2. Distribute the copies of **"Sweet History: The Story of Hot Chocolate"**.

3. Students should read the passage carefully. Once they are finished reading, they should answer questions on the comprehension sheet. Students should refer back to the passage for information.

Students who may require additional support: _____

Additional Notes: _____

E. Independent Reading Book Response, Start Time_____, End Time_____

In this activity, students will read their chapter books (novels) independently, and then respond to the book using writing prompts.

1. Distribute the **Independent Reading Book Response** sheets.

2. Inform students that after reading quietly in their books for _____ minutes, they will respond by answering prompts on their own sheets of paper.

3. Distribute the **Independent Reading Book Response Sheets**. Read through the prompts and example with the students. Note to students that (like the example) they should use complete sentences and include examples or quotes from their book to support their answers whenever possible.

Lesson Plans, continued

Students who may require additional support: _____

Additional Notes:_____

F. ABC Chart, Start Time_____, End Time_____

In this activity, students will fill out an alphabetical chart with vocabulary words or other important terms from a selection of reading.

1. Distribute the two-sided ABC Chart. Inform students that after reading a passage, they will show what they've learned by recording important information on their charts.

2. Students should read pages _____ in their _____ books.

3. Students should read (choose one):

☐ independently   ☐ with assigned partners   ☐ with student-chosen partners

☐ in small groups   ☐ as a whole class

4. After students have completed reading, they should begin completing the chart with important terms from the text.

5. Students should complete at least ____ squares on the chart. See sample below.

A	B	C
	basalt is a rock made from lava that cools quickly	coal and claystone are examples of sedimentary rocks
D diorite is an igneous rock	**E** erosion is a process that breaks down rocks	**F**

Students who may require additional support: _____

Additional Notes: _____

9

G. Monkey On My Back Spelling Practice, Start Time_____, End Time_____

In this activity, students practice their weekly Spelling words with a partner, using a fun "Monkey Sheet".

1. Inform students that they will be practicing their Spelling words with partners, using an activity called "Monkey On My Back". Explain to students that the term "monkey on my back" refers to something that's bothersome or a burden, especially for a long period of time. For example, you might say, "My mom makes me rake leaves every Saturday before I can go play. That chore is a real monkey on my back!"

2. Explain that sometimes, not knowing Spelling words (especially if there's a test coming up), can feel like having a monkey on your back, too. With today's activity, students will practice their Spelling words, and thus, get the monkeys off their backs.

3. Students should begin with a copy of this week's **Spelling words**, a partner, a pencil, and a **Monkey Sheet**.

4. Partner 1 gives Partner 2 a word to spell. Partner 2 must correctly spell the word aloud while Partner 1 checks the spelling from the list. If Partner 2 spells the word correctly, he or she gets to cross one monkey off his or her sheet. If Partner 2 spells the word wrong, he or she cannot cross off a monkey, but should instead copy the word onto the **Monkey Sheet** for additional practice later.

5. Repeat Step 4 until one partner crosses off all the monkeys from his or her sheet. Students who spelled words incorrectly should take their **Monkey Sheets** home for review.

6. Students may play the game with (choose one):

☐ student-chosen partners   ☐ assigned partners

Students who may require additional support:_____

Additional Notes:_____

Plan in a Can: 4th-5th Grade: Fall and Winter Theme

Copyroom Quick Guide

Make Copies of the Following: **Number of Copies:**

Fall Festival Math Practice
3 Pages

Secret Code Multiplication and Division
2 Pages, Back to Back

Scrambled Sentences Activity
2 Pages, Single Sided

"Sweet History" Hot Chocolate Reading Passage
2 Pages, Back to Back

"Sweet History" Hot Chocolate Comprehension Questions
1 Page

Independent Reading Book Response
1 Page

ABC Chart for Content Areas
2 Pages, Back to Back

Monkey On My Back Spelling Practice
1 Page, 2 Per Game Cards Per Sheet

Commonly Misspelled Words: Spelling List
1 Page, 2 Lists Per Sheet

Also Copy: _____

Fall Festival Math Practice

Mathematician _____

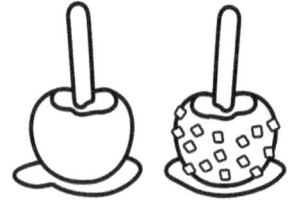

Solve the problems below. Read carefully. Show your work on seperate pieces of paper.

1. For the Fall party, Olivia needs enough hot chocolate for 45 people. Boxes of hot chocolate come in packs of 6 servings.

a. How many boxes of hot chocolate will Olivia need to buy in order to have one serving of hot chocolate for everyone at the party?

b. How many servings will be left over?

2. Emily and Andre both purchased packages of caramel apples for the school's Fall Festival. One of them bought caramel apples that came in packs of 8. One bought apples that came in packs of 6. Emily bought at total of 128 caramel apples. Andre bought a total of 108 caramel apples.

a. Which kid bought caramel apples in packs of 8 and which kid bought apples in packs of 6?

b. How many packs did each kid buy?

3. At the Fall Festival, Anthony volunteered to work the pie stand. He has 14 pies. He needs to cut the pies to make 84 slices. How many pieces should Anthony cut in each pie?

4. Jack volunteered for the face painting booth at the Fall Festival. For each face he paints, he will use .25 ounces of paint.

a. If 120 students get their faces painted, how many ounces of paint will Jack use in all?

b. If face paint comes in 8 ounce bottles, how many bottles should Jack buy in order to have enough paint for 120 faces?

5. Hot apple cider is sold at the beverage booth for .75 cents per cup. Hot chocolate is sold for $1.25 per cup. How much money did the beverage booth make in all if they sold 82 cups of apple cider and 96 cups of hot chocolate?

6. Brian's dad is making his famous pumpkin bread for the festival's bake sale. However, he needs to bake two loaves, instead of just one. His recipe is below. Double the measurements for all of the ingredients and write the new recipe on the card. Give your answer in reduced fractions or mixed numbers.

Single-Loaf Recipe	Double-Loaf Recipe
3 1/2 cups all-purpose flour	_____ cups all-purpose flour
1 1/4 teaspoons baking soda	_____ teaspoons baking soda
1 1/4 teaspoons salt	_____ teaspoons salt
3/4 teaspoon baking powder	_____ teaspoon baking powder
1/4 teaspoon ground nutmeg	_____ teaspoon ground nutmeg
1/2 teaspoon ground allspice	_____ teaspoon ground allspice
1 1/2 teaspoon ground cinnamon	_____ teaspoon ground cinnamon
1/2 teaspoon ground cloves	_____ teaspoon ground cloves
1 1/3 cups white sugar	_____ cups white sugar
2/3 cup canola oil	_____ cup canola oil
4 eggs, beaten	_____ eggs, beaten
1 3/4 cups mashed pumpkin	_____ cups mashed pumpkin
2/3 cup water	_____ cups water

13

7. The festival has a rectangular maze made out of bales of hay. The outside of the maze is 24 hay bales long and 29 hay bales wide. Each bale of hay is 3 feet long. What is the perimeter of the hay maze? (Helpful hint: Draw and label a picture first!)

8. Will is in charge of the "Bobbing for Apples" game. He placed a total of 20 apples in a tub of water. Complete the chart below to show what fraction and percent of the total apples in the tub each variety of apples represents.

Variety of Apple	Number of Apples	Reduced Fraction	Percent of Total Apples
Fuji	1	$\frac{1}{20}$	5%
Jonathan	3		
Pink Lady	4		
Red Delicious	4		
Honeycrisp	8		

Secret Code Division and Multiplication

Name: _____

What to do: Solve the multiplication and division problems in parentheses below. Each number stands for a letter in the key. Plug in the letters to find the answer to each question.

Key

A=1 B=2 C=3 D= 4   E=5 F=6   G=7   H=8 I=9 J=10

K=11 L=12 M=13 N=14 O=15 P=16 Q=17 R=18 S=19

T=20   U=21 V=22 W=23   X=24 Y=25   Z=26

Q: Why do penguins swim in salt water?

A: ___ ___ ___ ___ ___ ___   ___ ___ ___ ___ ___
(48-3) (25 ÷ 5) (4x4) (32 ÷ 2) (35÷ 7) (6x3)   (46÷2) (12÷12) (4x5) (45÷9) (36÷2)

___ ___ ___ ___ ___   ___ ___ ___ ___
(26÷2) (7÷7) (33÷3) (30÷6) (38÷2)   (60÷3) (40÷5) (15÷3) (13x1)

___ ___ ___ ___ ___ ___!
(38÷2) (28÷2) (25÷5) (40÷8) (13x2) (50÷10)

Q: What do you get when you cross a snowman with a shark?

A: ___ ___ ___ ___ ___ ___ ___ ___ ___!
(36÷6) (9x2) (30÷2) (19x1) (80÷4) (28÷14) (3x3) (60÷3) (25÷5)

15

Scrambled Sentences!

Sentence Sorter: _____

The following sentences belong in a three-paragraph essay about hedgehogs. However, the sentences have been shaken-up and are totally out of order. Here's what you should do:

1. Read each sentence.
2. Cut them out.
3. Arrange them in an order than makes sense.
4. Be sure to separate the sentences into three paragraphs.
5. Neatly glue the sentences to a separate sheet of paper.

Helpful Hints:

1. Watch for topic sentences. The first sentence of a paragraph should tell you what the paragraph will be about without adding too many details.

2. Remember, the first paragraph of an essay often gives the reader an idea about what the rest of the essay will say. Think about this when you are putting your paragraphs in order.

Now for the scrambled sentences!

1	Also, a hedgehog's spines are filled with air pockets, which may help cushion them in short falls or help them float if they need to travel a short distance across water.

2	Then, the hedgehog will chew this mouthful of smelly matter and mix it with its own saliva to make a frothy substance.

3	Hedgehogs' spines usually only fall out when they shed their baby spines in exchange for adult-size spines.

4	These unique creatures were first given the name "hedgehog" around the year 1450.

5	Next, the hedgehog will lick its own back in order to spread this mixture over its body and annoint itself.

| 6 | A hedgehog is a spiny mammal that lives in parts of Europe, Asia, Africa, and New Zealand. |

| 7 | The smell might come from a strong-smelling plant, soil, or other material. |

| 8 | "Hedge" is another term for the shrubs and bushes where these animals live, and "hog" is for their upturned, pig-like nose. |

| 9 | When it is threatened, a hedgehog may curl into a ball and use the muscles on its back to cover itself in raised spines and keep predators from attacking. |

| 10 | In other words, it's harder for predators to find a hedgehog they can't smell! |

| 11 | A hedgehog's quills are not designed to come out of its skin. |

| 12 | Hedgehogs are nocturnal and live on a diet of mostly insects, but their diet can include other sources of food. |

| 13 | Scientists aren't sure why hedgehogs anoint themselves, but many think anointing helps the hedgehog cover up its own scent and smell like its surroundings instead. |

| 14 | In fact, the hedgehog's closest living relatives are small, furry shrews. |

| 15 | Hedgehogs often rely on their 5,000-6,000 spines to protect them from predators. |

| 16 | When a hedgehog finds a new smell in its surroundings, it takes a few bites of the source of the smell. |

| 17 | A hedgehog's quills are made of keratin, the same substance that makes up our hair and fingernails. |

| 18 | Although they both have many spines, hedgehogs are not actually related to porcupines. |

| 19 | One of a hedgehog's most unique features are its stiff, hollow spines or quills. |

| 20 | Hedgehogs have a rather unusual habit called **anointing** (uh-noyn-ting), which may help them avoid predators. |

Sweet History: The Story of Hot Chocolate

by Eve Drueke

There's much more to this favorite wintertime drink than you might think!
Read on to find out more about hot chocolate's rich history.

What is hot chocolate made of? Chocolate or cocoa powder, sugar, milk, and a dash of world history. That's right--this favorite wintertime treat is rich with history from across the globe, starting nearly 2,000 years ago.

A Bitter Beginning

The first drinks made with cocoa were most likely created 2,000 years ago by the Mayas, in what is now Columbia. However, the first versions of hot chocolate were quite different from the drink we enjoy with a few marshmallows today. The earliest forms of chocolate drinks contained chocolate from cacao beans, vanilla, and other spices, including chilli peppers, and was served cold. Sugar had not yet been brought to Mayan culture. As a result, the earliest chocolate drinks were unsweetened and tasted quite strong and bitter.

The chocolate drink was formed by mixing a paste of mashed cacao beans with cornmeal, chilli, and other spices, and then poured back and forth between two cups until a froth was formed.

This beverage wasn't enjoyed by ancient Mayans as a way to warm up after playing in the snow. In fact, people often drank it to cure stomach aches and stuffy noses.

The earliest versions of hot chocolate tasted nothing like the drink we enjoy today.

Cocoa Catches On

Over several hundred years, the idea of a chocolate drink spread from the Maya to the Aztec people, who lived in what is now Mexico. By the 1500's, chocolate drinks were being served both hot and cold, though no one is certain when the beverage started being heated.

In 1528, the Spanish conquistador* Hernan Cortés returned to Spain after invading the civilizations in Mexico and Peru. On his return trip home, Cortés brought cocoa beans and equipment for making the chocolate drink back to Europe with him. This is when the beginnings of what is now hot chocolate was introduced to Europe.

*conquistador: one of the Spanish warriors who took over Mexico and Peru in the 1500's.

A Royal Treat

After hot chocolate was introduced to Europe, it slowly became more popular. King Charles V and other nobles began enjoying the beverage. The fact that the king drank hot chocolate helped make the drink popular with wealthy people. At that time, it was very difficult for anyone who wasn't rich to afford hot chocolate. Cocoa beans had only yet been found in South America, and shipping the beans across the Atlantic Ocean was very expensive.

At this time, chocolate candy still had not been invented in Europe. Because this chocolate drink was the only version of chocolate that was known in Europe, people simply called it "chocolate", instead of "hot chocolate". If you traveled back in time and asked for "chocolate" and expected a candy bar, you'd get a bitter liquid surprise!

Sweet at Last!

At the end of the 1600's, hot chocolate underwent changes that made the drink taste more like the beverage so many people enjoy today. Sugar was added to the hot chocolate, making it no longer bitter. A doctor who disliked hot chocolate realized it tasted much better when it was mixed with milk. The practice of adding milk and sugar to chocolate and spices caught on, and soon, a sweet, creamy version of hot chocolate became very popular, especially among wealthy people and royalty. The very first "chocolate house", a cafe made just for serving hot chocolate, was opened in 1657.

Hold the (Cocoa) Butter

In 1828, a Dutch inventor named Coenraad Johannes van Houten (Kon-rad Yo-hah-nis van How-ten) created a special machine called a **cocoa press** that helped chocolate become even tastier. Inside a cacao pod is an oily substance called **cocoa butter**. Too much cocoa butter can make chocolate feel oily and taste greasy. The new machine invented by van Houten separated the oily cocoa butter from the rest of the cacao seeds. When cocoa butter is removed, a rich and flavorful cocoa powder is left. The dry cocoa powder is used for baking or inside dry mixes of hot chocolate. Something else happened once cocoa powder could be separated from cocoa butter. People found that mixing a little bit of cocoa butter with a lot of cocoa powder made a delicious form of chocolate that could be shaped into bars!

Cocoa in Every Country

Hot chocolate has undergone many different changes since it was first created nearly 2,000 years ago. Although all versions of modern hot chocolate are now sweet, the way hot chocolate is made and served still changes from place to place.

In Columbia, where hot chocolate first began, the drink is made with milk and served with bread and cheese for breakfast. Some types of hot chocolate served in Italy, Spain, and Germany are very thick. If you order hot chocolate at a cafe in Belgium, you might receive a hot bowl of milk with chocolate chips to melt in it.

However you prefer to drink it, the next time you take a sip of this favorite chocolate beverage, think about how much history is inside your cup of cocoa!

Sweet History: The Story of Hot Chocolate
Reading Comprehension Questions

Name: _____

Read and answer the questions below.
Use the passage to find information or examples when needed.

1. Describe two ways in which hot chocolate today is different than the chocolate drink first created by the Mayans.

_____

_____

2. Name one of the Mayans' reasons for drinking chocolate mixed with chilis and spices.

_____

_____

3. How was the chocolate drink brought to Europe? What helped make it popular?

_____

_____

4. Describe one way the invention of the cocoa press changed how chocolate was prepared.

_____

_____

5. Compare the way you make or drink hot chocolate to the way it is served in another country. Be sure to name the country you are using for comparison.

_____

_____

Independent Reading Response: What's Happening in Your Book?

Book Reviewer: _____

1. Write a **4-5 sentence summary** of what happened in part of the story you read today. Be sure to describe all the characters that were included in this part of the story.

2. **Why were these events important?** Think about how they have changed the story, could set the story up for a change in the plot, or affected the characters in the story.

3. **Choose the most important character** from the pages you read today. Describe what you think his or her thoughts or feelings may be. Be sure to explain why you think he or she felt that way. You may want to use proof from the book, such as a character's action or words.

For example, you might write something like: "**The most important character from Chapter 12 was Jane. I believe she felt proud and excited when she stood up to the neighborhood bully, Christine. The book gives proof that Jane feels proud when it says, "Jane stood at the corner, watching Christine walk away. Jane stood tall, her hands on her hips, her chin up, and shoulders back. She couldn't hide her smile as she thought to herself, "I can't believe I actually made Christine the Mean Machine apologize."**

4. **What do you predict will happen** in the story next? What parts of the story helped you make your prediction?

5. What is your **personal response** to the part of the book you read today? Did you like it, love it, find it uninteresting, or were you on the edge of your seat with excitement? Explain what made you feel this way.

6. **What do you wonder** about this part of the story? Your question could be about something that was confusing, like, "I wonder what Christine meant when she said, 'I'll make quick work of you,'". Your question could also be about the characters, story, or even the author's ideas, such as, I wonder why Christine is so mean, or I wonder why Christine never gets in trouble for her bullying.

7. Based on what you've read so far, **how many stars would you give this book**, on a scale from 1-5? A score of one star means, "I really don't like it". A score of five stars means, "I love it!". Why would you give it that rating? Would you recommend this book to a friend? Why or why not?

Journal Notes:

As you read, use the space below to jot down any important ideas or details!

The ABC's of: _____ By: _____

A	B	C
D	E	F
G	H	I
J	K	L

23

M	N	O
P	Q	R
S	T	U
V	W/X	Y/Z

Monkey On My Back Game Sheets

Player: _____

🐵	🐵	🐵	🐵
🐵	🐵	🐵	🐵
🐵	🐵	🐵	🐵
🐵	🐵	🐵	🐵
🐵	🐵	🐵	🐵
🐵	🐵	🐵	🐵
🐵	🐵	🐵	🐵
🐵	🐵	🐵	🐵

Words to Practice:

_____

_____

_____

_____

Player: _____

🐵	🐵	🐵	🐵
🐵	🐵	🐵	🐵
🐵	🐵	🐵	🐵
🐵	🐵	🐵	🐵
🐵	🐵	🐵	🐵
🐵	🐵	🐵	🐵
🐵	🐵	🐵	🐵
🐵	🐵	🐵	🐵

Words to Practice:

_____

_____

_____

_____

Spelling List: Commonly Misspelled Words

Commonly ~~Mispelled~~ (Misspelled) Words

1. different
2. because
3. believe
4. calendar
5. library
6. restaurant
7. there (*a place; "over there"*)
8. their (*belongs to them; "their dog"*)
9. they're (*short for "they are"*)
10. until
11. weird
12. weather
13. choose
14. chose
15. losing

Bonus: sincerely

Name: _____

Commonly ~~Mispelled~~ (Misspelled) Words

1. different
2. because
3. believe
4. calendar
5. library
6. restaurant
7. there (*a place; "over there"*)
8. their (*belongs to them; "their dog"*)
9. they're (*short for "they are"*)
10. until
11. weird
12. weather
13. choose
14. chose
15. losing

Bonus: sincerely

Name: _____

Fall Festival Math Practice

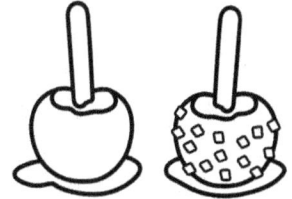

Mathematician <u>Key</u>

Solve the problems below. Read carefully. Show your work on seperate pieces of paper.

1. For the Fall party, Olivia needs enough hot chocolate for 45 people. Boxes of hot chocolate come in packs of 6 servings.

a. How many boxes of hot chocolate will Olivia need to buy in order to have one serving of hot chocolate for everyone at the party?

48 is the multiple of 6 that's closest to 45 (without being too small). 48/6 = 8. 48 - 45 = 3. Olivia will need 8 boxes.

b. How many servings will be left over?

Olivia will have 3 packets left over.

2. Emily and Andre both purchased packages of caramel apples for the school's Fall Festival. One of them bought caramel apples that came in packs of 8. One bought apples that came in packs of 6. Emily bought at total of 128 caramel apples. Andre bought a total of 108 caramel apples.

a. Which kid bought caramel apples in packs of 8 and which kid bought apples in packs of 6?

Emily bought packs of 8 caramel apples, because her total of 128 apples is divisible by 8 and not 6. Andre bought packs of 6 caramel apples, because his total of 108 apples is divisible by 6 and not 8.

b. How many packs did each kid buy?

Emily bought 16 packs (128/8 = 16) and Andre bought 18 packs (108/6 = 18).

3. At the Fall Festival, Anthony volunteered to work the pie stand. He has 14 pies. He needs to cut the pies to make 84 slices. How many pieces should Anthony cut in each pie?

84/14 = 6 slices per pie

4. Jack volunteered for the face painting booth at the Fall Festival. For each face he paints, he will use .25 ounces of paint.

a. If 120 students get their faces painted, how many ounces of paint will Jack use in all?

.25 x 120 = 30 ounces of paint

b. If face paint comes in 8 ounce bottles, how many bottles should Jack buy in order to have enough paint for 120 faces?

4 bottles. 8 x 4 = 32 ounces. 3 bottles would only have 24 ounces, which is not enough paint.

27

5. Hot apple cider is sold at the beverage booth for .75 cents per cup. Hot chocolate is sold for $1.25 per cup. How much money did the beverage booth make in all if they sold 82 cups of apple cider and 96 cups of hot chocolate?

.75 x 82 cups = $61.50

$1.25 x 96 cups = $120.00

$61.50 + $120.00 = $181.50

6. Brian's dad is making his famous pumpkin bread for the festival's bake sale. However, he needs to bake two loaves, instead of just one. His recipe is below. Double the measurements for all of the ingredients and write the new recipe on the card. Give your answer in reduced fractions or mixed numbers.

Single-Loaf Recipe	Double-Loaf Recipe
3 1/2 cups all-purpose flour	7 cups all-purpose flour
1 1/4 teaspoons baking soda	2 1/2 teaspoons baking soda
1 1/4 teaspoons salt	2 1/2 teaspoons salt
3/4 teaspoon baking powder	1 1/2 teaspoon baking powder
1/4 teaspoon ground nutmeg	1/2 teaspoon ground nutmeg
1/2 teaspoon ground allspice	1 teaspoon ground allspice
1 1/2 teaspoon ground cinnamon	3 teaspoon ground cinnamon
1/2 teaspoon ground cloves	1 teaspoon ground cloves
1 1/3 cups white sugar	2 2/3 cups white sugar
2/3 cup canola oil	1 1/3 cup canola oil
4 eggs, beaten	8 eggs, beaten
1 3/4 cups mashed pumpkin	3 1/2 cups mashed pumpkin
2/3 cup water	1 1/3 cups water

7. The festival has a rectangular maze made out of bales of hay. The outside of the maze is 24 hay bales long and 29 hay bales wide. Each bale of hay is 3 feet long. What is the perimeter of the hay maze? (Helpful hint: Draw and label a picture first!)

318 feet total perimeter

3 feet x 29 bales x 2 sides = 174 feet. 3 feet x 24 bales x 2 sides = 144 feet

174 + 144 = <u>318</u>

8. Will is in charge of the "Bobbing for Apples" game. He placed a total of 20 apples in a tub of water. Complete the chart below to show what fraction and percent of the total apples in the tub each variety of apples represents.

Variety of Apple	Number of Apples	Reduced Fraction	Percent of Total Apples
Fuji	1	$\frac{1}{20}$	5%
Jonathan	3	$\frac{3}{20}$	15%
Pink Lady	4	$\frac{1}{5}$	20%
Red Delicious	4	$\frac{1}{5}$	20%
Honeycrisp	8	$\frac{2}{5}$	40%

29

Secret Code Division and Multiplication

Name: Key

What to do: Solve the multiplication and division problems in parentheses below. Each number stands for a letter in the key. Plug in the letters to find the answer to each question.

Key

A=1 B=2 C=3 D= 4 E=5 F=6 G=7 H=8 I=9 J=10

K=11 L=12 M=13 N=14 O=15 P=16 Q=17 R=18 S=19

T=20 U=21 V=22 W=23 X=24 Y=25 Z=26

Q: Why do penguins swim in salt water?

A:
P   E   P   P   E   R   W   A   T   E   R
(48-3) (25 ÷ 5) (4x4) (32 ÷ 2) (35÷ 7) (6x3)   (46÷2) (12÷12) (4x5) (45÷9) (36÷2)

M   A   K   E   S   T   H   E   M
(26÷2) (7÷7) (33÷3) (30÷6) (38÷2)   (60÷3) (40÷5) (15÷3) (13x1)

S   N   E   E   Z   E !
(38÷2) (28÷2) (25÷5) (40÷8) (13x2) (50÷10)

Q: What do you get when you cross a snowman with a shark?

A:
F   R   O   S   T   B   I   T   E !
(36÷6) (9x2) (30÷2) (19x1) (80÷4) (28÷14) (3x3) (60÷3) (25÷5)

Scrambled Sentences: Answer Key

Note: A few sentences may fit logically in more than one place. It's most important that sentence placement reflects an understanding that a beginning paragraph breifly introduces ideas, while the remaining paragraphs focus on one main idea.

Sentence Order Quick Guide:
In the correct order, sentences are in the following sequence, with some variation allowed.
Paragraphs two and three can be switched.
Pargraph 1: 6, 18, 14, 12, 4, 8
Paragraph 2: 19, 17, 11, 3, 15, 9, 1
Paragraph 3: 20, 16, 7, 2, 5, 13, 10

A hedgehog is a spiny mammal that lives in parts of Europe, Asia, Africa, and New Zealand. Although they both have many spines, hedgehogs are not actually related to porcupines. In fact, the hedgehog's closest living relatives are small, furry shrews. Hedgehogs are nocturnal and live on a diet of mostly insects, but their diet can include other sources of food. These unique creatures were first given the name "hedgehog" around the year 1450. "Hedge" is another term for the shrubs and bushes were these animals live, and "hog" is for their upturned, pig-like nose.

One of a hedgehog's most unique features are its stiff, hollow spines or quills. A hedgehog's quills are made of keratin, the same substance that makes up our hair and fingernails. A hedgehog's quills are not designed to come out of its skin. Hedgehogs' spines usually only fall out when they shed their baby spines in exchange for adult-size spines. Hedgehogs often rely on their 5,000-6,000 spines to protect them from predators. When it is threatened, a hedgehog may curl into a ball and use the muscles on its back to cover itself in raised spines and keep predators from attacking. Also, hedgehog's spines are filled with air pockets, which may help cushion them in short falls or help them float if they need to travel a short distance across water.

Hedgehogs have a rather unusual habit called anointing, which may help them avoid predators. When a hedgehog finds a new smell in its surroundings, it takes a few bites of the source of the smell. The smell might come from a strong-smelling plant, soil, or other material. Then, the hedgehog will chew this mouthful of smelly matter and mix it with its own saliva to make a frothy substance. Next, the hedgehog will lick its own back in order to spread this mixture over its body and annoint itself. Scientists aren't sure why hedgehogs anoint themselves, but many think anointing helps the hedgehog cover up its own scent and smell like its surroundings instead. In other words, it's harder for predators to find a hedgehog they can't smell!

Sweet History: The Story of Hot Chocolate
Reading Comprehension Questions

Name: _Key_

Read and answer the questions below.
Use the passage to find information or examples when needed.

1. Describe two ways in which hot chocolate today is different than the chocolate drink first created by the Mayans.

Modern hot chocolate is served warm and sweet. The chocolate drink created by

Mayans was cold, bitter, and sometimes made with cornmeal.

2. Name one of the Mayans' reasons for drinking chocolate mixed with chilis and spices.

The chocolate drink created by the Mayans was thought to cure stuffy noses and help

digestion.

3. How was the chocolate drink brought to Europe? What helped make it popular?

The chocolate drink was introduced to Spain by Cortes, the Spanish conquistador. King

Charles V drank chocolate, which made it grow in popularity among royals and the wealthy.

4. Describe one way the invention of the cocoa press changed how chocolate was prepared.

The cocoa press separated oily cocoa butter from cacao seeds, which left behind a more flavorful cocoa

powder. Removing cocoa butter also meant chocolate could be molded into bars and candy.

5. Compare the way you make or drink hot chocolate to the way it is served in another country. Be sure to name the country you are using for comparison.

Answers vary.

32

Plan in a Can!: Fall and Winter Theme: Common Core State Standards Alignment

Fall Festival Math fulfills the following standards, in whole or in part:

Fourth Grade:

CCSS.MATH.CONTENT.4.NBT.B.5
Multiply a whole number of up to four digits by a one-digit whole number, and multiply two two-digit numbers, using strategies based on place value and the properties of operations. Illustrate and explain the calculation by using equations, rectangular arrays, and/or area models.

CCSS.MATH.CONTENT.4.NBT.B.6
Find whole-number quotients and remainders with up to four-digit dividends and one-digit divisors, using strategies based on place value, the properties of operations, and/or the relationship between multiplication and division. Illustrate and explain the calculation by using equations, rectangular arrays, and/or area models.

CCSS.MATH.CONTENT.4.NBT.B.4
Fluently add and subtract multi-digit whole numbers using the standard algorithm.

CCSS.MATH.CONTENT.4.OA.A.3
Solve multistep word problems posed with whole numbers and having whole-number answers using the four operations, including problems in which remainders must be interpreted. Represent these problems using equations with a letter standing for the unknown quantity. Assess the reasonableness of answers using mental computation and estimation strategies including rounding.

CCSS.MATH.CONTENT.4.MD.A.2
Use the four operations to solve word problems involving distances, intervals of time, liquid volumes, masses of objects, and money, including problems involving simple fractions or decimals, and problems that require expressing measurements given in a larger unit in terms of a smaller unit. Represent measurement quantities using diagrams such as number line diagrams that feature a measurement scale.

CCSS.MATH.CONTENT.4.NF.B.3.D
Solve word problems involving addition and subtraction of fractions referring to the same whole and having like denominators, e.g., by using visual fraction models and equations to represent the problem.

CCSS.MATH.CONTENT.4.NF.B.4.C
Solve word problems involving multiplication of a fraction by a whole number, e.g., by using visual fraction models and equations to represent the problem.

Fifth Grade:

CCSS.MATH.CONTENT.5.NBT.B.5
Fluently multiply multi-digit whole numbers using the standard algorithm.

CCSS.MATH.CONTENT.5.NBT.B.6
Find whole-number quotients of whole numbers with up to four-digit dividends and two-digit divisors, using strategies based on place value, the properties of operations, and/or the relationship between multiplication and division. Illustrate and explain the calculation by using equations, rectangular arrays, and/or area models.

CCSS.MATH.CONTENT.5.NBT.B.6
Find whole-number quotients of whole numbers with up to four-digit dividends and two-digit divisors, using strategies based on place value, the properties of operations, and/or the relationship between multiplication and division. Illustrate and explain the calculation by using equations, rectangular arrays, and/or area models.

CCSS.MATH.CONTENT.5.NF.B.3
Interpret a fraction as division of the numerator by the denominator ($a/b = a \div b$). Solve word problems involving division of whole numbers leading to answers in the form of fractions or mixed numbers, e.g., by using visual fraction models or equations to represent the problem.

CCSS.MATH.CONTENT.5.NF.B.7.C
Solve real world problems involving division of unit fractions by non-zero whole numbers and division of whole numbers by unit fractions, e.g., by using visual fraction models and equations to represent the problem.

"Sweet History: The Story of Hot Chocolate" fulfills the following standards, in whole or in part:

Fourth Grade:

CCSS.ELA-LITERACY.RI.4.1
Refer to details and examples in a text when explaining what the text says explicitly and when drawing inferences from the text.

CCSS.ELA-LITERACY.RI.4.3
Explain events, procedures, ideas, or concepts in a historical, scientific, or technical text, including what happened and why, based on specific information in the text.

CCSS.ELA-LITERACY.RI.4.10
By the end of year, read and comprehend informational texts, including history/social studies, science, and technical texts, in the grades 4-5 text complexity band proficiently, with scaffolding as needed at the high end of the range.

Fifth Grade:

CCSS.ELA-LITERACY.RI.5.1
Quote accurately from a text when explaining what the text says explicitly and when drawing inferences from the text.

CCSS.ELA-LITERACY.RI.5.3
Explain the relationships or interactions between two or more individuals, events, ideas, or concepts in a historical, scientific, or technical text based on specific information in the text.

CCSS.ELA-LITERACY.RI.5.7
Draw on information from multiple print or digital sources, demonstrating the ability to locate an answer to a question quickly or to solve a problem efficiently.

CCSS.ELA-LITERACY.RI.5.10
By the end of the year, read and comprehend informational texts, including history/social studies, science, and technical texts, at the high end of the grades 4-5 text complexity band independently and proficiently.

Secret Code Multiplication and Division fulfills the following standards, in whole or in part:

Fourth Grade:

CCSS.MATH.CONTENT.4.NBT.B.5
Multiply a whole number of up to four digits by a one-digit whole number, and multiply two two-digit numbers, using strategies based on place value and the properties of operations. Illustrate and explain the calculation by using equations, rectangular arrays, and/or area models.

Fifth Grade:

CCSS.MATH.CONTENT.5.NBT.B.5
Fluently multiply multi-digit whole numbers using the standard algorithm.

Scrambled Sentences Activity fulfills the following standards, in whole or in part:

Fourth Grade:

CCSS.ELA-LITERACY.RI.4.2
Determine the main idea of a text and explain how it is supported by key details; summarize the text.

CCSS.ELA-LITERACY.RI.4.5
Describe the overall structure (e.g., chronology, comparison, cause/effect, problem/solution) of events, ideas, concepts, or information in a text or part of a text.

CCSS.ELA-LITERACY.RI.4.10
By the end of year, read and comprehend informational texts, including history/social studies, science, and technical texts, in the grades 4-5 text complexity band proficiently, with scaffolding as needed at the high end of the range.

CCSS.ELA-LITERACY.W.4.1.A
Introduce a topic or text clearly, state an opinion, and create an organizational structure in which related ideas are grouped to support the writer's purpose.

CCSS.ELA-LITERACY.W.4.4
Produce clear and coherent writing in which the development and organization are appropriate to task, purpose, and audience.

Fifth Grade:

CCSS.ELA-LITERACY.RI.5.2
Determine two or more main ideas of a text and explain how they are supported by key details; summarize the text.

CCSS.ELA-LITERACY.RI.5.5
Compare and contrast the overall structure (e.g., chronology, comparison, cause/effect, problem/solution) of events, ideas, concepts, or information in two or more texts.

CCSS.ELA-LITERACY.RI.5.7
Draw on information from multiple print or digital sources, demonstrating the ability to locate an answer to a question quickly or to solve a problem efficiently.

CCSS.ELA-LITERACY.W.5.2.A
Introduce a topic clearly, provide a general observation and focus, and group related information logically; include formatting (e.g., headings), illustrations, and multimedia when useful to aiding comprehension.

CCSS.ELA-LITERACY.W.5.4
Produce clear and coherent writing in which the development and organization are appropriate to task, purpose, and audience.

Independent Reading Response fulfills the following standards, in whole or in part:

Fourth:

CCSS.ELA-LITERACY.RL.4.1
Refer to details and examples in a text when explaining what the text says explicitly and when drawing inferences from the text.

CCSS.ELA-LITERACY.RL.4.3
Describe in depth a character, setting, or event in a story or drama, drawing on specific details in the text (e.g., a character's thoughts, words, or actions).

CCSS.ELA-LITERACY.RL.4.10
By the end of the year, read and comprehend literature, including stories, dramas, and poetry, in the grades 4-5 text complexity band proficiently, with scaffolding as needed at the high end of the range.

Fifth:

CCSS.ELA-LITERACY.RL.5.1
Quote accurately from a text when explaining what the text says explicitly and when drawing inferences from the text.

CCSS.ELA-LITERACY.RL.5.2
Determine a theme of a story, drama, or poem from details in the text, including how characters in a story or drama respond to challenges or how the speaker in a poem reflects upon a topic; summarize the text.

CCSS.ELA-LITERACY.RL.5.10
By the end of the year, read and comprehend literature, including stories, dramas, and poetry, at the high end of the grades 4-5 text complexity band independently and proficiently.

Monkey On My Back Spelling fulfills the following standards, in whole or in part:

Fourth:

CCSS.ELA-LITERACY.L.4.1.G
Correctly use frequently confused words (e.g., to, too, two; there, their).*

CCSS.ELA-LITERACY.L.4.2.D
Spell grade-appropriate words correctly, consulting references as needed.

Fifth:

CCSS.ELA-LITERACY.L.5.2.E
Spell grade-appropriate words correctly, consulting references as needed.